G. B. Trudeau

CHECK YOUR EGOS AT THE DOOR

A Doonesbury book

First published in Great Britain in Abacus by
Sphere Books Ltd 1986
27 Wright's Lane, London W8 5SW
Copyright © 1984, 1985 by G. B. Trudeau

The author and publisher gratefully acknowledge the following companies
that contributed time and material to make this book possible:
Abington Display Company, Inc.; Alling and Cory; Color Associates, Inc.;
The Lehigh Press, Inc.; Phoenix Color Corporation.

Printed and bound in Great Britain by
Collins, Glasgow

G. B. Trudeau's *Doonesbury* is featured
including *The Guardian*. It is still the only c
the Pulitzer Prize (1975), and, in addition, G. B. Trudeau has received
thirteen honorary degrees. The musical *Doonesbury: A Musical Comedy*
(1983; for which he wrote the book and lyrics) was nominated for four
Drama Desk Awards, including Outstanding Lyrics and Outstanding Book
in a Musical. A recent animated feature shown on NBC TV was nominated
for an Academy Award.

Also by G. B. Trudeau in Abacus:

THAT'S *DOCTOR SINATRA*, YOU LITTLE BIMBO

MIKE, WHY IS REAGAN EVEN BOTHERING WITH BLACK VOTERS? HE HARDLY NEEDS THEM.

WELL, CASSIE SAYS HIS PEOPLE WANT TO BROADEN HIS MANDATE..

10-17

THEY'RE ALSO TRYING TO COUNTER A NEW NONPARTISAN STUDY THAT'S FOUND THAT BLACKS OF ALL CLASSES ARE DRAMATICALLY WORSE OFF AS A RESULT OF REAGAN POLICIES.

I'M SUPPOSED TO COME UP WITH A SLOGAN THAT MAKES THE POINT THAT REAGAN HAS IGNORED ALL THE DISADVANTAGED, NOT BLACKS PER SE.

"REAGAN: HE'S NO RACIST."

THAT'S JUST A ROUGH DRAFT. I WANT TO PLAY AROUND WITH IT SOME MORE.

GOOD EVENING. VICE PRESIDENT GEORGE BUSH'S MANHOOD PROBLEM SURFACED AGAIN TODAY, AS CONCERN OVER HIS LACK OF POLITICAL COURAGE CONTINUED TO GROW.

CAMPAIGN OFFICIALS, ALARMED BY REACTION TO BUSH'S NUMEROUS POLICY REVERSALS, HAVE PERSUADED HIM TO TAKE SWIFT ACTION TO PREVENT FURTHER EROSION OF HIS INTEGRITY.

ACCORDINGLY, IN A WHITE HOUSE CEREMONY TODAY, BUSH WILL FORMALLY PLACE HIS EMBATTLED MANHOOD IN A BLIND TRUST.

IT WILL BE RESTORED TO HIM ONLY IN TIMES OF NATIONAL EMERGENCY.

GB Trudeau

GO AHEAD, ZONKER. TELL J.J. WHAT YOU JUST TOLD ME.

J.J., YOUR WORRIES ARE OVER. I'VE DECIDED TO GO TO MED SCHOOL.

UH-HUH. AND I'M JOINING THE BOLSHOI.

I'M SERIOUS, J.J. –I'VE APPLIED TO THE BABY DOC COLLEGE OF PHYSICIANS, THE FINEST NEW MED SCHOOL IN ALL OF HAITI!

AND I DON'T WANT TO SOUND COCKY OR ANYTHING, BUT I HAVE EVERY REASON TO BELIEVE THAT I'M A SHOO-IN!

GB Trudeau

I DON'T KNOW, SIR. I'VE NEVER SEEN GRADES LIKE THESE.

I DON'T CARE, DEAN HONEY. WE NEED HIM TO SHORE UP THE VOLLEYBALL SQUAD!

..AND CALL THE LABOR MINISTRY. WE'RE GOING TO NEED SCABS TO SERVE LUNCH AFTER THE CEREMONY.

THAT WON'T BE NECESSARY, SIR. I SETTLED THE KITCHEN WORKER STRIKE LAST NIGHT.

YOU DID? NOW, THAT'S THE BEST NEWS I'VE HAD ALL WEEK! GOOD WORK, HONEY!

THANK YOU, SIR. I WONDER IF YOU'D LIKE TO GO THROUGH THE LIST OF TODAY'S HONORARY DEGREE RECIPIENTS.

SURE, WHY NOT? LET'S SEE.. PAUL LUMIÈRE. JEANNE GENOT. PIERRE BERGER. ADRIENNE D'ARCY. IMPRESSIVE LINE-UP, HONEY!

YES, SIR.

WHO THE HELL ARE THEY?

THE KITCHEN STAFF.

@BTrudeau

LISTEN TO THIS, RICK. "REAGAN ALSO RECEIVED 61% OF THE ELDERLY VOTE, 56% OF THE YOUTH VOTE, AND 67% OF THE YUPPIE VOTE"!

DUANE, WHY ARE YOU STILL TORTURING YOURSELF WITH ELECTION RESULTS? IT'S OVER, MAN.

RICK, IN THE LAST EIGHT YEARS, I'VE HANDLED SYMBOLS FOR CARTER, BROWN AND MONDALE. I'M NOT EXACTLY ON A WINNING STREAK. I'VE GOT TO FIGURE OUT WHERE WE WENT WRONG!

I STILL CAN'T HELP FEELING THAT ALL WE NEEDED THIS FALL WAS ONE BREAK, SOMETHING THAT WOULD'VE DRAMATIZED THE CASE AGAINST REAGAN.

LIKE WHAT?

I DUNNO. A NUCLEAR WAR OR SOMETHING.

BY GOD, *THAT* WOULD HAVE DONE IT! I'LL BET YOU WOULD HAVE SWEPT BOTH HOUSES!

YOU MARK?

THAT'S RIGHT. WHO ARE YOU?

I'M SPANKY LEE JAMES. I'M THE ENGINEER ON YOUR NEW SHOW. WELCOME TO NPR.

HERE'S THE DEAL. AT THIS HOUR OF THE NIGHT, WE HAVE A SMALL BUT DEVOTED CALL-IN AUDIENCE. THEY ARE EDDIE, MEL, ROSITA, COL. HARWOOD, AND SOME GUY NAMED "CHICKENBONE" FROM CHICAGO.

THAT'S IT?

PRETTY MUCH. IF EDDIE CALLS, TRY TO KEEP HIM OFF J. EDGAR HOOVER.

GBTrudeau

SO WHERE ARE THE BEST GRATES, ALICE?

WELL, THE SAFEST IS #1, RICKY. IT'S RIGHT IN FRONT OF THE D.C. POLICE HEADQUARTERS. IT'S DRY HEAT, TOO, NOT STEAM.

STEAM HEAT'S A PROBLEM?

YOU KIDDING? IT'LL SOAK YOU THROUGH IN TWO MINUTES.. HEY! WHY ARE YOU WRITING THIS DOWN?

UM..ALICE, I'VE EXPLAINED IT TO YOU THREE TIMES. I'M WRITING A PIECE ON THE HOMELESS..

AND YOU WANT TO KNOW THE WHOLE TRASHY STORY OF HOW I ENDED UP LIKE THIS!

WELL, NO, NOT IF..

IT ALL STARTED AT MY DEBUTANTE PARTY..

BOY, IT'S GREAT TO SEE YOU AGAIN, UNCLE DUKE. IT'S BEEN MUCH TOO LONG!

SURE HAS. GOT THE CERTIFIED CHECK FOR YOUR TUITION?

YUP. HERE YOU GO. I HOPE THIS WORKS OUT. DAD HAD TO TAKE OUT A PRETTY STIFF LOAN..

HE WON'T REGRET IT, BOY. HE'LL BE WATCHING YOU GRADUATE IN THREE SHORT YEARS! FOUR YEARS, MAX.

I DUNNO, UNCLE DUKE. I'VE NEVER EVEN TAKEN BIO BEFORE.

NEITHER HAVE A LOT OF OUR STUDENTS. DEAN HONEY HERE IS TUTORING HALF THE VOLLEYBALL TEAM!

VOLLEYBALL? THERE'S TIME FOR VOLLEYBALL?

MOST OF THE GAMES ARE FIXED, BUT IT'S STILL GOOD FUN.

WELCOME TO CLUB PRE-MED, SIR!

© B. Trudeau

AND THEN WHAT?

WELL, ONCE I BOUGHT THE BROTHEL, I GOT THE LOCAL AUTHORITIES TO RAZE MOST OF THE SURROUNDING SHANTIES.

AFTER THAT, IT WAS JUST A MATTER OF PUTTING IN THE TENNIS COURTS AND SENDING OUT BROCHURES. THE REST IS OFF-SHORE EDUCATION / HISTORY!

IT'S AN AMAZING STORY, UNCLE DUKE, SIMPLY AMAZING!

THANKS. WELL, I BETTER GET BACK TO THE O.R. I WAS IN THE MIDDLE OF SURGERY WHEN YOU CALLED.

SURGERY? BUT.. BUT YOU'RE NOT A DOCTOR.

I KNOW, BUT IT'S AN EMERGENCY. AND OUR REGULAR CUTTER IS OUT SNORKELING.

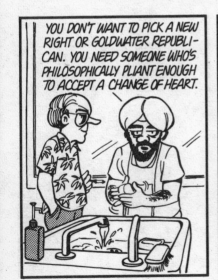

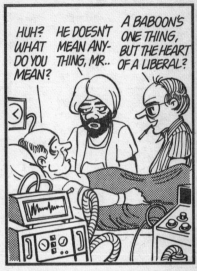

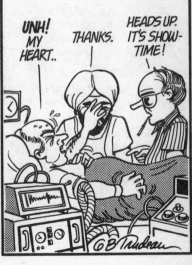

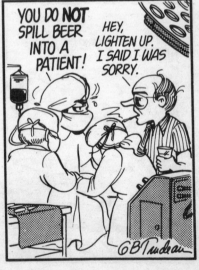

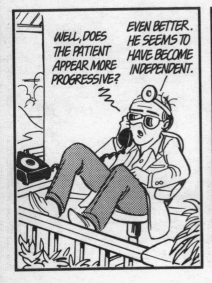

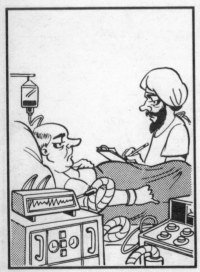

TODAY A COALITION OF FARM BELT SENATORS PROPOSED A "WAY-OF-LIFE" LOAN PROGRAM TO SHORE UP THE NATION'S AILING FAMILY FARMS..

ALARMED BY THE ADMINISTRATION'S ANTI-SUBSIDY RHETORIC, BILL SPONSOR CHARLES GRASSLEY SAID THE WAY-OF-LIFE LOANS WOULD BE USED TO REFINANCE AN IMPORTANT PART OF AMERICA'S HERITAGE.

SENATOR, HOW WILL YOU DETERMINE WHETHER A FARM FAMILY IS ELIGIBLE FOR A WAY-OF-LIFE LOAN?

WELL, FIRST THEY MUST PROVE THEY STILL MAKE THEIR OWN CORNBREAD..

FROM SCRATCH?

YOUR MOM'S TESTIFYING BEFORE CONGRESS?

YUP. THE AGRICULTURE COMMITTEE. OUR SENATOR LINED HER UP.

APPARENTLY, HE REALLY BELIEVES SHE CAN HELP GENERATE SOME SYMPATHY FOR HIS WAY-OF-LIFE REFINANCING PROGRAM.

WHAT DO YOU THINK SHE'LL SAY?

I SHUDDER TO THINK. MOM'S BEEN THROUGH SOME PRETTY TOUGH TIMES, BUT SHE CAN LAY IT ON A LITTLE THICK.

STATE YOUR NAME, PLEASE.

THE WIDOW DOONESBURY.

GB Trudeau

SENATOR, I REALIZE THERE'S A COMING SHAKEDOWN IN THE FARM ECONOMY, AND THAT THIS ADMINISTRATION WON'T DO MUCH TO CUSHION THE BLOW.

BUT THE FACT REMAINS I'M THE WIDOW OF A WORLD WAR II VETERAN, I'M THE MOTHER OF TWO, I BAKE APPLE PIE, AND I LIVE ON A FAMILY FARM! THAT SHOULD **COUNT** FOR SOMETHING!

I YIELD TO THE WITNESS'S AWESOME ICONOGRAPHY.

YOU BETTER.

GBTrudeau